World Issues

GENOCIDE

Alex Woolf

Chrysalis Children's Books

WORLD ISSUES

Animal Rights
Drugs
Equal Opportunities
Genetic Engineering
Genocide
Human Rights
Poverty
Racism
Refugees
Terrorism

First published in the UK in 2003 by
Chrysalis Children's Books
64 Brewery Road, London N7 9NT

Editor: Clare Weaver
Editorial Manager: Joyce Bentley
Designer: Mark Whitchurch
Consultant: John Polley
Picture Researcher: Glass Onion Pictures

ISBN: 1 84138 877 7

British Library Cataloguing in Publication Data for this book is available from the British Library.

A BELITHA BOOK

Printed in Hong Kong/China
10 9 8 7 6 5 4 3 2 1

Picture Acknowledgements
We wish to thank the following individuals and organizations for their help and assistance, and for supplying material in their collections: AKG London 3, 10 (Heinrich Hoffman), 13 (Erich Lessing), 14, 19, 20, 39, 47; Art Archive 12 (Dagli Orti); Camera Press 5 top (Fiona McDougall), 7, 30 (Benoit Gysembergh), 32 (SRDJ), 38 (Andy Eames), 42 (Paul Harris); Corbis 1 (Michael Freeman), 4 (Peter Turnley), 23 (Bettmann), 25 (Bettmann), 26 (Bettmann), 27 (Bettmann), 29 (Michael Freeman), 36 (Gregor Schmid), 41 (Galen Rowell); David King Collection 24; Exile Images 35 (H Davies), 40 (R Chalasani); Mary Evans Picture Library 8; Popperfoto 5 bottom (AFP/Joel Robine), 9 (Reuters), 11, 17, 18, 21 (AFP), 28, 31 (Hocine Zaqurar), 33 (Reuters), 37 (AFP/Ramzi Haydar), 43 (Reuters), 44 (Reuters), 45 (Reuters), 46 (Reuters); Rex Features 5 middle (Action Press), 16 (Sipa), 34 (Sipa); Topham Picturepoint *front cover* (Image Works), 6 (Image Works), 15 (Fotomas), 22. The pictures used in this book do not show the actual people named in the case studies in the text.

CONTENTS

Muhamed's Story

Muhamed Cehajic was a victim of genocide – the deliberate attempt to destroy a whole community. He was just one of many thousands of people who were caught up in the appalling events that took place in Bosnia, a province of the former country of Yugoslavia, between 1991 and 1995. This is his story.

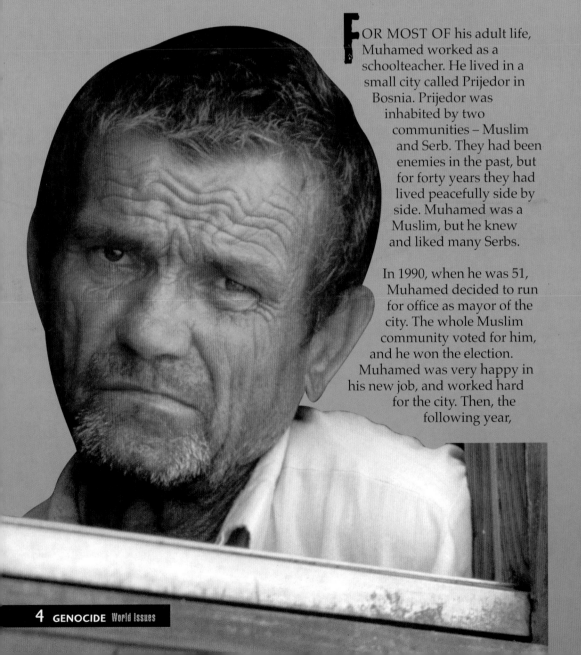

FOR MOST OF his adult life, Muhamed worked as a schoolteacher. He lived in a small city called Prijedor in Bosnia. Prijedor was inhabited by two communities – Muslim and Serb. They had been enemies in the past, but for forty years they had lived peacefully side by side. Muhamed was a Muslim, but he knew and liked many Serbs.

In 1990, when he was 51, Muhamed decided to run for office as mayor of the city. The whole Muslim community voted for him, and he won the election. Muhamed was very happy in his new job, and worked hard for the city. Then, the following year, catastrophe struck. Civil war broke out in Yugoslavia, and the country began to fall apart. The Serbs of Bosnia wished to remain part of Yugoslavia, while the Muslims wanted the province to become independent. Old tensions resurfaced and, almost overnight, the two communities became bitter enemies.

In early 1992, Serb army forces took control of Prijedor. They ordered Muhamed to go on the radio and tell the people of the city to surrender their weapons to the Serbs. Instead, Muhamed told the citizens to remain calm and to use peaceful means to resist the illegal Serb government.

Prison camp

Muhamed was removed from his job as mayor, and later arrested by Serb police. He was sent to a prison camp in a nearby city called Omarska. Prisoners at Omarska slept on the floor, and were fed one meal a day – a slice of bread and a bowl of thin soup. Conditions were filthy, and lice infested the prisoners' hair and beards. They were regularly tortured and beaten, and many did not survive.

Muhamed was held at Omarska for five weeks. Then, one night towards the end of July 1992, he and six others – all high-ranking men from Prijedor – were led away by guards. They were never seen again. Muhamed was killed for no other reason than because he was a Muslim, and a leader of his community. Sadly, his story is not unusual.

Source: A Witness to Genocide: The First Inside Account of the Horrors of Ethnic Cleansing in Bosnia by Roy Gutman

Other communities at risk

Muhamed is just one of the many victims of genocide found all over the world.

BURUNDI
In Burundi, in central Africa, the Tutsi and Hutu tribes have been in conflict since 1996, during which time over 200 000 people have been killed. Many experts are fearful that the majority Hutus may begin massacring the Tutsis.

IRAQ
In 1988, the Iraqi government carried out a genocide against the Kurdish people. Up to 100 000 people may have died. Since then, the Kurds of Iraq have continued to be persecuted by the Iraqi government as victims of imprisonment, torture and murder.

CHECHNYA
The Chechen people of central Asia have been fighting for their independence from Russia since 1999. Many hundreds of Chechen prisoners have disappeared, and human rights groups fear that Russian troops are carrying out a genocide.

What Is Genocide?

Genocide is any action aimed at the destruction of a group of people, such as a nation, an ethnic group, or a race. An ethnic group is a community who shares a similar culture or background, and a race is a group of people who share similar physical characteristics, such as skin or hair colour.

THE TERM 'GENOCIDE' was invented in 1944 by a Polish-American legal expert named Raphael Lemkin. He decided a new word was needed to describe the large-scale, deliberate massacres that the Nazis were carrying out against the Jews and other ethnic or national groups at that time living in occupied Europe (those countries invaded and ruled by the Nazis). Lemkin combined the Greek word 'genos', meaning race or tribe, and 'cide' from the Latin word for killing.

Ever since the word was created, there has been a debate about its exact meaning, and about what it should include. Some have argued that the term

These skulls in Rwanda, central Africa, mark the site of a massacre of Tutsis by Hutus during a genocide that took place there in 1994. The government has left the skulls there to remind people of what happened.

The United Nations in session. Despite passing a law against genocide, the UN has been unable to stop genocidal massacres taking place in the years since 1948.

DEBATE - Should the definition of genocide be widened to include other kinds of mass killing?

- Yes. All mass killing is equally bad. Its seriousness should not depend on whether the victims form a particular group.
- No. There is a danger if you widen the definition too far, the word might lose its power.

should include only actions that cause death. Others believe that the destruction of culture, religion and language are also serious crimes worthy of being called genocide. There are also arguments over what kinds of groups can be considered victims of genocide. As well as national, ethnic and racial groups, some insist that political groups or economic classes can also suffer a genocidal attack.

How is genocide defined?

The United Nations (UN), an organization of countries formed after World War II, passed a law in 1948 making genocide illegal. The UN defined 'genocide' as any act committed with intent to destroy in whole or in part a national, ethnic, racial or religious group. This included the following kinds of activity:

- Killing members of the group.
- Causing serious bodily or mental harm to members of the group.
- Deliberately inflicting on the group conditions of life calculated to bring

about its physical destruction in whole or in part.
- Imposing measures intended to prevent births within the group.
- Forcibly transferring children of the group to another group.

According to this definition, the attempt to destroy a political movement or economic class would not be classed as genocide. Cases such as these may, however, be prosecuted as 'crimes against humanity'. The UN also limited the definition to physical or psychological attacks, and did not include acts that attack a group's cultural or religious identity.

In this illustration from a children's book published in Nazi Germany, a Jewish couple are shown as being fat and rich. This is an example of the 'classification' of a victim group.

What are the six stages of genocide?

Genocides occur for many different historical and political reasons, but they tend to have certain features in common. Researchers have attempted to identify these common features in the hope that this might increase the chances of predicting and preventing them in the future. Genocide expert Dr Gregory Stanton, has suggested there are six stages in the build-up to a genocide:

1. Classification. A government or group wishing to carry out a genocide will first classify who is included in the group they wish to destroy. Classification can be on the basis of physical appearance, for example, or religion.

2. Symbolization. The next stage is the development of symbols, which are used to identify the victim group and to mark them out physically, such as the yellow star that Jews were forced to wear in Nazi Germany.

3. Dehumanization. In the third stage, the victim group is no longer thought of as human beings. Members of the group are likened to animals, vermin, or

diseases, to make the idea of murdering them seem less abnormal.

4. Organization. Unlike a massacre, a genocide is generally planned and organized. Special units may need to be armed and trained to carry out the attacks.

5. Polarization. The victim group is physically separated from the rest of the population. Laws may forbid intermarriage or social interaction.

6. Preparation. The victim group is placed in camps, or forced into areas where they cannot grow food or sustain themselves. Death lists are drawn up. This stage occurs immediately before the genocide itself.

Not all these stages have to happen. Some potential genocides may never progress beyond stages two or three. However, Stanton's analysis – and others like it – provides governments and international observers with a useful guide to help them monitor potential genocides around the world.

Blue scarves

An example of the 'symbolization' stage in the build-up to a genocide occurred in Cambodia in 1975. The Cambodian government, known as the Khmer Rouge, had decided that the people of the 'Eastern Zone' (provinces in eastern Cambodia) were enemies of the people and should be relocated and eliminated. To mark them out, they issued every man, woman and child with a blue-and-white-checked scarf, known as a *kroma*. The Khmer Rouge insisted that Eastern Zone people wear these scarves at all times.

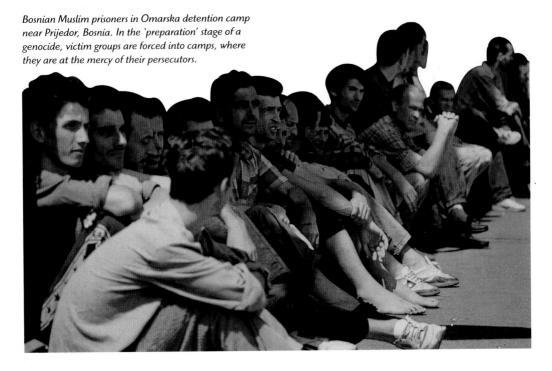

Bosnian Muslim prisoners in Omarska detention camp near Prijedor, Bosnia. In the 'preparation' stage of a genocide, victim groups are forced into camps, where they are at the mercy of their persecutors.

On the night of 9–10 November 1938, the Nazis organized a general attack on Jewish homes, businesses and synagogues throughout Germany. The Jewish community was ordered to pay for the damage. The night was known as Kristalnacht (Crystal Night) because of all the broken glass.

What was the Holocaust?

The Holocaust was the attempt by Nazi Germany to wipe out the Jews of Europe. Around six million Jews were killed out of an estimated total population of eight million. There have been other genocides before and since, but the Holocaust remains a unique event in history. For the first time, the full power of a modern industrial state was used to transport, enslave and slaughter an entire people.

The Nazi Party, under Adolf Hitler's leadership, took power in Germany in 1933. They were fiercely anti-Semitic (prejudiced against Jews). They blamed the Jews for all of Germany's problems, such as defeat in World War I and economic depression. In fact, German Jews were very supportive of their country, and many had fought in the German army in World War I.

The Nazis introduced laws to separate the Jews from the rest of society, preventing them from marrying, socializing or working with other Germans. Propaganda was used to persuade the population that Jews were dangerous and not to be trusted. World War II began in 1939 and the German occupation of Poland brought millions of Jews under Nazi control. Jews were separated from the rest of the population by being made to live in rundown areas called ghettos.

In 1941, following the German invasion of the Soviet Union, the Nazis began massacring thousands of Jews and burying them in mass graves. That year, the Nazis secretly decided to exterminate all European Jews. Death camps were built in Poland, at Auschwitz, Chelmno, Belzec, Sobibor, Treblinka and Majdanek. Millions of Jews were transported to these camps from all over occupied Europe. Most were killed with poisonous gas, and their bodies were then burned. The Holocaust was only stopped when the Nazis were defeated by the Allies in 1945.

A clear conscience

During the Nazi invasion of the Soviet Union, execution squads followed the advancing German army, massacring the Jewish population of captured towns. An eyewitness recalls events in a small Ukrainian town in August 1941: 'For about two hours some three hundred men, including children aged fourteen, were seized in the streets or driven from their homes... The Germans did not take part in the abductions. This was carried out with clear conscience by our Ukrainian neighbours who had lived side by side with the Jews for generations... The job of shooting the victims was performed by the German murderers, whose superior training prepared them for it. At six o'clock in the evening the whole thing was over.'

Source: Never Again: A History of the Holocaust *by Martin Gilbert*

After the liberation of Buchenwald concentration camp in 1945, citizens from a nearby town were made to come and look at some of the terrible acts that had been carried out there.

Has There Always Been Genocide?

Throughout history, peoples have been massacred, enslaved or deported – either by their own leaders, or by outside conquerors. Genocides were generally planned in advance and carefully organized, but they also often occurred as a by-product of war and conquest. For example, in ancient times it was common for captured cities or towns to be burned to the ground and their inhabitants massacred.

BETWEEN 1100 AND 600 BC, the Assyrians used what might be described as genocidal methods for maintaining control of their empire in the Middle East. They slaughtered thousands of prisoners of war as sacrifices to their supreme god. Those who rebelled against their rule were beheaded, impaled on stakes or thrown alive into giant ovens. In 722 BC, the Assyrians captured the land of Israel, and deported the whole population to Mesopotamia (a region covering what is now Iraq, and parts of Turkey and Syria).

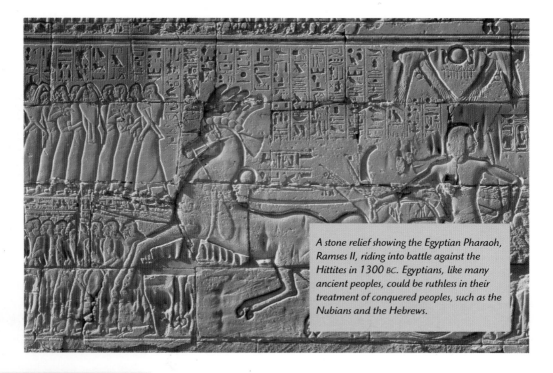

A stone relief showing the Egyptian Pharaoh, Ramses II, riding into battle against the Hittites in 1300 BC. Egyptians, like many ancient peoples, could be ruthless in their treatment of conquered peoples, such as the Nubians and the Hebrews.

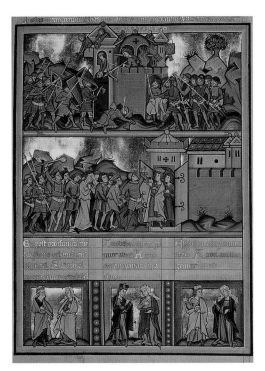

A medieval illustration showing the Jews being led into captivity by the Babylonians in the sixth century BC, following the destruction of Jerusalem. The Jews have often been victims of persecution throughout their history.

In the fifteenth century AD, the Aztecs of Mesoamerica sacrificed many thousands of war prisoners to their gods. In 1490, some 20 000 victims were killed to celebrate the completion of a new pyramid. The line of doomed people was said to have stretched three kilometres outside the city. After it was over, the stench of rotting flesh hung over the city for weeks.

The persecution of minorities living within a larger community is another common event in history. Many Christians were killed under the Roman emperor Nero. According to a Roman historian, Nero covered them in the skins of wild animals and had them torn apart by dogs, or he used them as human torches to light the gardens of his palace. In the Middle Ages, Christian Europe was also intolerant of minorities. Jewish communities were frequently the victims of massacres and, in 1492, the Muslims were expelled from Spain.

The Roman destruction of Carthage

Carthage was a powerful city-state on the coast of North Africa between the sixth and third centuries BC. From 264 BC, it became involved in a series of wars with the rival city-state of Rome. By 149 BC, Carthage had lost all its colonies, and the Roman army had lain siege to the city itself. Carthage held out for three years before finally surrendering. The Romans stormed into the city and began massacring its population. The killing lasted six days. By the time they were finished, only about 50 000 Carthaginians, out of an original population of 250 000, remained alive. They were sold into slavery. The Romans burned the city to the ground, ripped up its stones and ploughed over the land in their determination that Carthage would never rise again.

The conquest of Mexico by the Spanish, led by Hernán Cortés. The European conquerors regarded the natives they encountered as inferior beings, and saw nothing wrong with driving them off their lands and enslaving them.

DEBATE - Did Europeans have the right to take over the lands of the native populations in America and Australasia?

• Yes. Without the pioneering efforts of those original explorers and settlers, countries like the USA and Australia would not exist today.

• No. The colonization of these lands caused the destruction of native cultures, some of them many thousands of years old. That cannot be right.

Did colonialism lead to genocide?

From the 1400s, European powers such as England, Spain, France and Portugal began to colonize various parts of the world. Their arrival in the Americas, Africa, the Pacific islands and Australasia brought disaster to the local populations. Although many natives died through mistreatment by their conquerors, by far the biggest killer was disease.

For example, the native population of the Americas was devastated by exposure to influenza, typhoid, measles and smallpox. They had no natural immunity to these diseases, and as a result suffered losses of up to 80 or 90 per cent of their original population. The natives of the West Indies were virtually wiped out in just a few generations.

The Europeans needed people to work on their plantations, but because so many natives died, they were forced to look elsewhere for labourers. In the mid-sixteenth century, Europeans began importing slaves from Africa to work in their American colonies. In the seventeenth century, two million slaves were transported from Africa to the Americas, and in the eighteenth century the figure rose to six million. At the height of the slave trade, some parts of west Africa were almost emptied of people.

Slaves were mostly captured by their fellow Africans, who sold them to European traders. Once bought, the slaves were branded like cattle and then herded on-board the ship. Conditions on the slave ships were appalling, and many died in the overcrowded, disease-ridden holds where they were held. Once in the New World (the Americas), slaves were sold once again, often at an auction. They then began their new life, usually as labourers on a plantation.

The African-American slave trade has been called a genocide because of the huge numbers of people deported, the dehumanizing way they were treated, and because so many died on the journey or soon after arrival. It has been called the 'African Holocaust'.

The Tasmanian Aborigines

In the early nineteenth century, the Aboriginal people of Tasmania were virtually wiped out by European settlers. The Europeans took Aboriginal lands, enslaved their women and killed many of their men. By 1835, only 135 out of an original population of about 4000 remained alive. A clergyman named George Robinson took the survivors to a small island to be 'Christianized'. All but 47 of them died. The 4000 Aborigines that live on Tasmania today are descendants of those 47 survivors.

Source: The Tasmanian Aboriginal People. A Nineteenth Century Genocide? A lecture by Dr Frank Chalk, Concordia University, Montreal, Quebec, Canada

A group of African men and boys being taken into slavery. Many slaves were in total despair on the long, uncomfortable voyage across the Atlantic Ocean. Some jumped overboard, preferring to die by drowning. Others refused to eat their rations.

What Are The Causes Of Genocide?

It is difficult for most people to imagine killing another human being, let alone taking part in a massacre. Yet genocides have occurred throughout history, and in many parts of the world. It is a mistake to believe that only certain peoples – usually in far-off lands – are capable of genocide. Under extreme enough circumstances, a genocide could occur anywhere.

GENOCIDES CAN SOMETIMES happen in countries where two or more peoples with a history of grievances live closely together. The dominant group may seize the opportunity, during a war or some other national crisis, to right perceived historic wrongs done to their people. In Rwanda, where a genocide took place in the 1990s, the Hutu majority strongly resented the Tutsi people. This resentment dated from before 1962, when the Tutsi had been the dominant tribe.

There was a similar underlying hostility between several of the ethnic groups in former Yugoslavia before civil war broke out in 1991. Serbs in the province of Kosovo claimed they were being mistreated by the Albanian Muslim majority. Serbs were also in the minority in Croatia, and many had died in massacres carried out by the pro-Nazi Croatian regime during World War II. The genocidal actions of the Serbs in the 1990s can partly be explained, but not justified, by pent-up hostility due to their treatment by other ethnic groups.

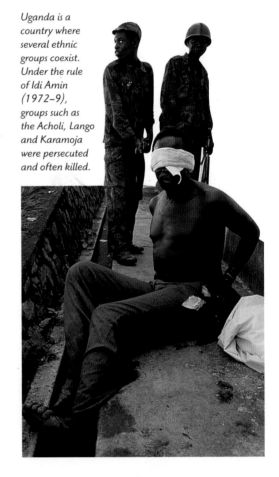

Uganda is a country where several ethnic groups coexist. Under the rule of Idi Amin (1972–9), groups such as the Acholi, Lango and Karamoja were persecuted and often killed.

Bodies from a mass grave are dug up for reburial in Chilgazi in Afghanistan – another divided country. This was the scene of a massacre of up to 8000 Hazara people in August 1998, carried out by the ruling Taliban, from the Pashtun tribe.

Genocide in Bangladesh

For nine months in 1971, the Bengali people of East Pakistan fought a successful war of independence against Pakistan, to form the new nation of Bangladesh. In the course of this war, the Pakistani army committed a genocide that resulted in the deaths of approximately 1.5 million people.

The Bengali nationalists had won an election in 1970, but the Pakistani authorities prevented them from taking power. So, the nationalists launched a non-violent protest. In March 1971, the Pakistani government decided it would try to terrify the Bengali population into submission.

They authorized the army to attack the Bengali capital of Dhaka. Thousands of unarmed civilians were killed in the city and surrounding countryside, and many homes and properties were destroyed.

The Pakistani forces targeted all able-bodied men, whether they were armed or not. During the campaign they also abducted and raped approximately 200 000 girls and women. Ten million Bengalis were forced to take refuge in neighbouring India. The killing finally ended in December when the Pakistanis were defeated by a combined Indian and Bengali army.

Prisoners in a Soviet labour camp engaged on a building project near Tiflis in Georgia in the 1930s. Most of these men were imprisoned for being from the wrong political class, or because they were suspected of opposing the Soviet regime.

Genocides have often occurred as a result of conquest. A conquering army may use genocide as a tool of repression. For example, in 1937, the Japanese army marched into the Chinese city of Nanking and murdered half of the city's population of 600 000. The leaders of an invading force may see genocide as the best means of bringing an occupied country, with a rebellious population, to submission. (See panel opposite about the Herero genocide in 1904.)

Most genocides are provoked by hatred of a racial or ethnic group arising out of conquest or historic grievances. However, several twentieth-century genocides have been motivated by a desire to create an ideal society. In these cases, the victims have been mainly political classes, who are seen as representing the 'old society' that must be destroyed. This was the background to many of the mass killings, persecutions and deportations in the Soviet Union under Stalin, in the People's Republic of China, and in Cambodia under the Khmer Rouge.

What conditions are needed for genocide?

For a genocide to occur, a number of conditions must usually exist. Firstly, there is often an extreme threat of some kind, such as an economic collapse or a war. The economic depression suffered by Germany in the early 1930s, or the invasion that occurred in Rwanda in the 1990s, are examples of this. In such circumstances, people can revert to primitive behaviour, believing they face a choice of 'kill or be killed'.

Genocide of the Hereros

In 1885, the Germans established a colony in Hereroland in south-west Africa. By 1903, the Herero tribe had grown increasingly bitter at their treatment by the Germans. Large areas of their land had been taken away, making it impossible for the Hereros to continue their traditional way of life.

In 1904, the Hereros rose against the Germans, attacking farms, villages and forts. Many of the colonists, including General von Trotha, the commander of the German forces, saw this uprising as an opportunity to wipe out the troublesome natives. The Hereros were easily defeated and forced back into the desert. The Germans pursued the fleeing tribe, poisoning the wells, and killing men, women and children indiscriminately.

After two years, just 20 000 Hereros remained out of an original population of 80 000. With their leaders all killed, the remaining Hereros were reduced to a state of virtual slavery by the Germans, and all but ceased to exist as a tribe.

German troops in East Africa under the command of Lothar von Trotha. In October 1904, von Trotha gave the following order: 'Any Herero found within the German borders with or without a gun, with or without cattle, will be shot'.

Adolf Hitler making a speech in 1937. Hitler and the other Nazi leaders hated the Jews and, when they took power in Germany, they were able to turn their anti-Semitism into government policy.

Secondly, there needs to exist a minority group within this threatened society that can, however illogically, be blamed for the crisis. The German Jews, for example, were accused of a whole range of sins in the 1920s and 30s, including growing rich on the miseries of others during the depression, plotting a communist revolution, and causing Germany's defeat in World War I. Some even believed there was a Jewish plot to take over the world. In Cambodia, where a genocide occurred during the 1970s, the city people were blamed by the peasants for keeping them in poverty by charging high interest on loans and paying low prices for their crops.

Thirdly, a genocide requires leadership. It cannot happen spontaneously. Someone needs to turn a general sense of anger and hatred into an organized policy of persecution and violence. Leaders like Adolf Hitler of Nazi Germany, Pol Pot of Cambodia and Chairman Mao of China were very clever at expressing people's fears, stirring up their emotions, and intensifying their loathing towards a particular group. Such leaders were able to make the target group appear less than human, and therefore easier to kill. Leaders who inspire genocides often encourage their followers in the belief that they themselves are the victims.

Whether their enemies are Jews, Muslims or Tutsis, the message is usually the same – they are the ones who are persecuting us.

The degree to which leaders actually cause genocides varies from case to case, and is often a matter of debate. Historians continue to argue over Hitler's involvement in the decision to exterminate the Jews. He issued no written order, and it is uncertain whether he even gave a verbal command to enact the final solution (Holocaust). Yet it was Hitler and his extreme anti-Semitism that was the major driving force behind the Nazi persecution of the Jews. Without him, it is difficult to imagine the Holocaust occurring.

A fourth condition required for a genocide to occur is organization. A leader acting alone cannot bring about a genocide. He needs loyal followers to carry out his wishes. People need to be armed and trained; victims need to be identified and segregated; methods of killing and disposal of bodies need to be established. All this requires planning and resources, which is why genocides are almost always carried out by governments. Usually only those in power have the ability to organize the systematic slaughter of large groups of people.

DEBATE - Under certain conditions, such as those discussed in this chapter, do you think anyone is capable of taking part in a genocide?

- Yes. Underneath, we are all essentially the same, and under extreme enough circumstances, any one of us could kill.
- No. If people are taught to respect other cultures, and to appreciate our common humanity, there is no reason why a genocide should ever occur.

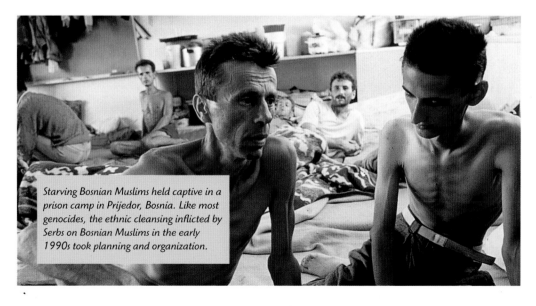

Starving Bosnian Muslims held captive in a prison camp in Prijedor, Bosnia. Like most genocides, the ethnic cleansing inflicted by Serbs on Bosnian Muslims in the early 1990s took planning and organization.

Where Has Genocide Occurred?

The twentieth century has been called the 'century of genocide'. The stories in this chapter are just a few of the major examples of mass killings that have taken place over the past hundred years. Although they occurred at different times and in different places, similar patterns emerge: ruthless leaders, the willingness of their subordinates to carry out orders, however brutal, and the helplessness of victims.

IN 1914, THE Muslim Ottoman Empire was in deep decline. It was ruled by a dictatorial regime known as the Young Turks. The Armenians, a Christian people living in an eastern region of the empire, wished for independence. They turned for support to France and Britain.

The Young Turks suspected these countries of wishing to take over parts of its empire, and they feared an alliance between the Armenians and the European powers. The solution to their problem, the Young Turks decided, would be to eliminate the Armenians. They found an opportunity, while Europe was preoccupied with World War I, to put their plan into action.

Beginning in April 1915, young, male Armenians were disarmed, placed in labour camps, and either worked to death or executed. Leading members of the Armenian community – among them doctors, lawyers, academics and clergymen – were arrested and taken away, never to be seen again.

An Armenian being hanged by Turks in Constantinople in 1915. To make the Armenian population more passive and obedient, the Turkish government first executed the adult male members of the community.

Orphan children, whose parents were killed in the genocide, are given bread at a refugee centre in Armenia. The Armenian nation was saved only by an American aid campaign, which raised millions of dollars to provide food and shelter for Armenian refugees.

Meanwhile, the rest of the population – mostly women, children and the elderly – were driven from their homes, and herded towards the Syrian desert. Some travelled by wagon or train, but most went on foot carrying only the barest essentials.

The intention of the deportations was to drive the Armenians out into remote, unprotected areas where they could be destroyed. Many were robbed of their possessions, and children were kidnapped. Others died of starvation, or were attacked by killing units who slaughtered them with swords, regardless of age or gender.

Only a quarter of the population survived the terrible journey. Many of those later died in the blistering heat of the desert. Others were butchered by killing units at a place called Deir el-Zor. In all, around one million Armenians died in the genocide of 1915–16.

An Armenian girl's story

Taki Levonian was fifteen at the time of the deportations. She and her family were forced to leave their home town of Keghi in May 1915. After six days they reached the town of Palu. There Taki's father was taken away. She never saw him again. The next day, her group was attacked by Turks and Kurds. Some got shot. Her aunt's husband was beaten in the head with an axe and his body dumped in the river. They walked on for fifteen days. There was little food and water. Their shoes had worn away, and Taki wrapped cloth around her bare feet to ease the pain. For three full days, they went without water. The children would cry 'water, water, water.' One of the children died.

Source: Century of Genocide: Eyewitness Accounts and Critical Views by Totten, Parsons and Charney (eds.)

Crimean Tatars are herded on to trains for deportation to distant places unknown to them. Men were separated from their wives and children, with barely any time to say goodbye, and little chance of ever seeing their families again.

Deportation of the Tatars

'Tatar homes were suddenly broken into by NKVD [secret police] agents ... armed with automatics. They dragged sleeping women, children and old people from their beds and, shoving automatics in their ribs, ordered them to be out of their homes within ten minutes... The agents ... swept through these homes, taking people's valuables, money, anything they liked, all the while calling the Tatars "swine", "scum", "damned traitors", and so on... In the locked, stifling freight cars, people began to die from hunger and illness. The NKVD troops would seize the corpses and throw them out of the freight car windows.'

Source: The Punished Peoples by Aleksander M. Nekrich

Who deported whole nations?

After the Nazi attack on the Soviet Union in 1941, the Soviet leader, Stalin, was concerned that some of the nationalities living within the Soviet Union may side with the invaders. Between late 1941 and the middle of 1944, eight nations, or ethnic groups, were deported: the Germans, Balkars, Chechens, Crimean Tatars, Ingushi, Karachai, Kalmyks and Meskhetians. In all, more than five million people were forced from their homes.

The deportations were carried out with brutal efficiency. Military units appeared in towns and villages announcing a 'transfer'. The population was given only a very brief time to collect a few belongings, before being put on trains. No exceptions were made, not even for families of those serving in the armed forces, or Communist Party members. They travelled in crowded, unsanitary conditions for hundreds of miles to remote regions in Kazakhstan, Siberia and Central Asia. Here they were made to work in mines, factories and on farms.

Many died on the journey, or soon after arrival, from hunger, cold and disease. The Crimean Tatars lost 46 per cent of their number in the first year and a half. About two-fifths of the Buddhist Kalmyks died by the end of the first year. Their original homes were looted and seized. Place names were changed, languages banned, and history rewritten, as if these peoples had never existed.

What was the rape of Nanking?

The Japanese invaded China in 1937. In December, after a four-day battle, they captured the ancient city of Nanking. For the Japanese, the first concern was to remove any threat from the 90 000 Chinese soldiers who had surrendered. The Japanese had been trained to believe that surrendering was a contemptible act of cowardice, so they viewed the Chinese soldiers as unworthy of life. The soldiers were driven in trucks to remote locations near the city. Here the Japanese butchered them in the most cruel and sadistic ways. Some were used for bayonet practice, or decapitated, while others were soaked in petrol and then set alight.

Chinese prisoners are used as live targets for bayonet practice by Japanese soldiers during the Japanese occupation of Nanking.

In Japan, the fall of Nanking – China's former capital city – was greeted with great enthusiasm by around 50 000 schoolboys, gathered in front of the Imperial Palace in Tokyo, waving flags and cheering.

The women of Nanking were the next Japanese target. More than 20 000 females, including elderly and pregnant women and young girls, were gang-raped by Japanese soldiers, then stabbed to death or shot. Throughout the city, soldiers fired their rifles into crowds of civilians, and set fire to buildings after locking people inside. Many Nanking residents were taken outside the city and forced to dig their own graves before being decapitated. Others were simply buried alive. This continued for six weeks, until the beginning of February 1938. Corpses could be seen everywhere. It is said that the streets ran red with blood.

A brave group of American and European doctors and missionaries, stationed in Nanking, managed to set up an international safety zone in the middle of the city. They frequently risked their lives by intervening to prevent an execution or a rape. About half the city's population of 600 000 took refuge in the safety zone. Almost all the others eventually perished.

The killing contest

When Tang Shunsan, a Nanking resident, was captured by the Japanese, he and a group of other prisoners were ordered to stand, several rows deep, in front of a freshly dug pit. The Japanese decided to have a contest to see who could kill the fastest. The soldiers split up into four teams of two, and began to behead the prisoners with their swords. The prisoners stood frozen with horror as their countrymen were slaughtered one by one. As the prisoner directly in front of Tang was decapitated, his body toppled backward against Tang, who was able to fall with it into the pit. Nobody noticed. Soon Tang was buried beneath headless bodies. Later, when the Japanese left the scene, Tang crawled out, and escaped. He was the only one to survive the killing contest.

Source: The Rape of Nanking: The Forgotten Holocaust of World War II by Iris Chang

Why were there massacres in Indonesia?

In the mid-1960s, the Indonesian Communist Party (PKI) looked to be on the verge of achieving power. It had a vast membership numbering millions, and exercised growing influence with the Indonesian government. It also had some powerful enemies: the Indonesian army was hostile to the PKI, because the party had its own military units, which were seen as a threat to the army's position. The Islamic community also feared a communist takeover, because the PKI might choose to make Indonesia a non-religious country.

In 1965, some extremists made an attempt to seize power in Indonesia. Some members of the PKI may have been involved, although this is not certain. At the time, however, most Indonesians believed that the communists were behind the attempted coup.

The ruins of the PKI headquarters in Jakarta, Indonesia, following an arson attack by anti-communist demonstrators. The sign on the right calls for the 'kidnappers to be put to death'. It refers to the seizure and assassination of six Indonesian generals, for which the PKI was blamed.

A few of the estimated 20 000 men, women and children, suspected of being enemies of the revolution, who were imprisoned by the Khmer Rouge in Cambodia. In a secret detention centre in Phnom Penh they were tortured, forced to write false confessions and then executed.

The anti-communist alliance of Muslims and the army took the opportunity to attack the PKI. Local Muslim leaders organized their followers into squads, and drew up lists of intended victims. The army helped by providing weapons and training. In some areas, the army itself carried out the attacks.

The massacres took place mostly at night. Victims were dragged from their beds, and taken to remote places outside their villages. They were killed with bayonets or parangs, which are single-bladed machetes used by Indonesian peasants. The bodies were dumped in rivers or buried in shallow graves. In most cases, the death squads killed only those named on their lists but, sometimes, whole villages associated with the PKI were slaughtered.

Approximately half a million people were killed in the massacres. As a result, the PKI was completely destroyed as a political force.

What happened in the 'killing fields'?

In 1975, a communist guerilla force, known as the Khmer Rouge, took power in Cambodia. Its leader, Pol Pot, planned a radical experiment to completely transform the country into a communist peasant farming society. He declared that Cambodia had to be purified of all foreign influences, including urban life, business and religion.

In the months that followed, Cambodia was gradually sealed off from the outside world. All foreigners were expelled, embassies were closed and foreign languages were banned. Newspapers and television stations were shut down, and mail and telephone usage was restricted. Money was prohibited, businesses closed down, and religion, education and public healthcare were all eliminated.

Cambodia's cities were then emptied of their inhabitants. They were forced from their homes and driven at gunpoint into the countryside. Two million were evacuated on foot from the capital city Phnom Penh, and as many as 20 000 died on the journey. The former city-dwellers, unused to farmwork, were forced to labour in the fields. They worked 18-hour days under the brutal supervision of armed soldiers, and were fed just one tin of rice every two days. Many thousands died of overwork, malnutrition and disease. The farms became known as the killing fields.

A peasant boy in Cambodia

Sat was a teenage peasant boy living in a small village in Cambodia under the Khmer Rouge. For five months in 1977, Sat and a hundred other boys were taken from their families to work on a rice farm. Every night there were meetings in which they were urged to work harder. Meals consisted of rice porridge with salt or fish. A month after starting, Sat was allowed to meet with his parents for a few hours. He never saw them again. Later they were put to work building a road. They worked, with short breaks, from 6am to 10pm. There were no rest days. Some of the boys fainted from exhaustion.

Source: Century of Genocide: Eyewitness Accounts and Critical Views by Totten, Parsons and Charney (eds.)

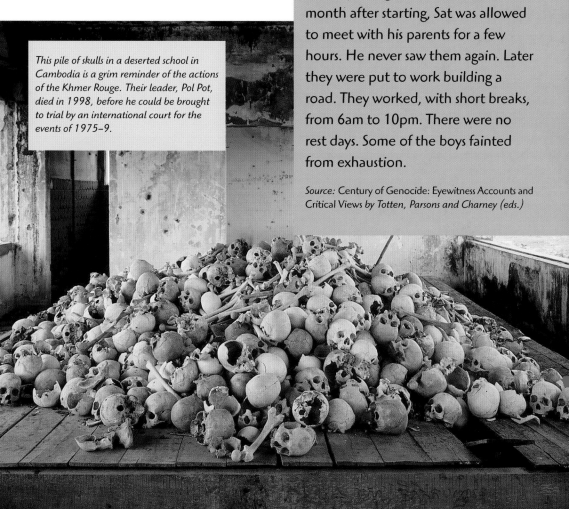

This pile of skulls in a deserted school in Cambodia is a grim reminder of the actions of the Khmer Rouge. Their leader, Pol Pot, died in 1998, before he could be brought to trial by an international court for the events of 1975–9.

Throughout the country, purges were carried out to destroy the educated elite of the 'old society'. Tens of thousands of doctors, lawyers, teachers, academics, Buddhist monks and officials of the old regime were all killed along with their families. The Khmer Rouge also attacked ethnic groups, including the Vietnamese, Chinese and Cham Muslims. Anyone suspected of being disloyal to Pol Pot, including many of the Khmer Rouge leaders, was shot. Up to 20 000 were tortured into giving false confessions of disloyalty, before being executed.

The Khmer Rouge was overthrown in 1979 following a Vietnamese invasion. Its four years in power had resulted in the deaths of approximately two million people – a quarter of the population.

What led to genocide in Rwanda?

Rwanda is a small country in central Africa, made up of two main ethnic groups (or tribes): the Hutus and the Tutsis. The Hutus form around 90 per cent of the population. Yet the Tutsis regard themselves as the elite, and during the period of Belgian rule (1916–62) the Tutsis had been the dominant tribe.

Following independence from Belgium, the Hutus seized power in Rwanda, and reversed the roles. Their persecution of the Tutsis caused 200 000 to flee to neighbouring countries. The Tutsis formed a guerrilla army, which, in 1990, invaded Rwanda. They forced the president to sign an agreement to allow the Tutsis to share power with the Hutus.

A refugee from the 1994 genocide in Rwanda. The wounds caused by ethnic hatred may take a very long time to heal. In the meantime, Rwandans face an uncertain future.

A Hutu remembers

Joseph Rukwavu, a Hutu, was 74 when the massacres took place. 'Two hundred were killed in my sector, even my wife, because she would not join Interahamwe [Hutu force responsible for the massacres]... The militia gathered everybody up near a big hole... They were weeping, even the men. Even the week before we killed them they were weeping in fear. They said, "Oh, we are the same people, we are your neighbours. Instead of hiding us you are killing us."'

Source: Mark Fritz, Associated Press, 13 May 1994

Young Hutus undergo military training in July 1994. Most of those who carried out the killings were farm labourers and unemployed city-dwellers. However, there were also a number of journalists, doctors, teachers and even priests who took part.

In April 1994, following the assassination of Rwanda's Hutu president, Hutu extremists, who had violently opposed power-sharing, went on the rampage, killing Tutsi leaders and moderate Hutu politicians. The violence spread into the countryside. Hutu military units, armed with machetes, clubs, guns and grenades, roamed around slaughtering Tutsi civilians. All Rwandans carried identification cards specifying their tribe, and these cards were now used to decide whether a person should live or die.

After ten Belgian peacekeepers were tortured and murdered by Hutus, Western countries began evacuating all their own citizens. UN peacekeepers were also withdrawn. However, no effort was made to evacuate Tutsi civilians, who were left without any protection from the murderous Hutu militias.

In an attempt to escape the killing, some Tutsis hid in churches, but these provided no refuge. In one church at Musha, 1200 Tutsis were killed in a massacre that lasted all day. Even the wounded, who managed to get to a hospital, were often sought out and murdered in their beds. Some were forced to kill their neighbours, and even members of their own families, to save their own lives.

The killings were only halted in July 1994 when Tutsis invaded from neighbouring countries, and defeated the Hutus. By then, around 800 000 people had been killed.

What was 'ethnic cleansing' in Bosnia?

Yugoslavia had existed as a unified state since World War II. However, by the 1980s, tensions between the country's different ethnic and religious groups – the Serbs, Croats and Muslims – began

to rise. The Serbs, under their new nationalist leader, Slobodan Milosevic, wished to unite the ethnic Serbs in the different regions of Yugoslavia to form a 'Greater Serbia'.

His plans were threatened when the province of Bosnia declared its independence from Yugoslavia in 1992. Most of Bosnia's population was Muslim, although it had a large Serbian minority who wished to remain part of Yugoslavia. Milosevic ordered the national army of Yugoslavia, which was dominated by Serbs, to attack Sarajevo, Bosnia's capital city. Serb snipers terrorized the city by shooting down civilians in the streets. There were many casualties, including 3500 children.

The Bosnian Muslims were no match for the Yugoslav army, and the Serbs gradually took control of the region. As each town was captured, they rounded

The Bosnian Serb leader Radovan Karadzic, accused of leading the slaughter of thousands of Bosnian Muslims and Croats. Karadzic (a former psychiatrist and poet) once said, 'Serbs and Muslims are like cats and dogs. They cannot live together in peace. It is impossible.'

Unidentified corpses, found in mass graves following the 1995 Srebrenica massacre, line the walls of a Bosnian morgue. The Bosnian Serb general, Radislav Krstic, who ordered the massacre, was found guilty of genocide in August 2002.

up the local Muslim population and either imprisoned them in concentration camps or, in some cases, massacred them. Women and girls were frequently the victims of rape. The plan was to turn Bosnia into a purely Serbian province. The process became known as 'ethnic cleansing'.

The Western powers tried through diplomatic means to bring the fighting to an end. Safe havens were established by the UN, but these were ignored by the Serbs. In one safe haven, at Srebrenica, a Serbian force rounded up 7500 Muslim men and boys between the ages of 12 and 60, and slaughtered them.

In response to this atrocity, a major NATO bombing campaign was launched, attacking Serb positions throughout Bosnia. The Serbs found

they had no choice but to negotiate. A peace deal was agreed. By this time, however, 200 000 Muslims had been massacred; over 20 000 were missing, feared dead; and two million Muslims had become refugees.

DEBATE - Is genocide ever inevitable (sure to happen)?

- Yes. If certain conditions arise, such as a hated minority, and an economic depression, a genocide is almost certain to follow.

- No. Genocides happen because of the actions of ruthless leaders. Social and economic factors cannot by themselves cause genocides to occur.

How Does The Media Report Genocide?

The media have a crucial role to play in alerting the world to a genocide. Photographs and television news reports can show in graphic terms what is happening. In Bosnia, a famous photo of a starving prisoner in a Serbian prison camp helped to focus the world's attention on the unfolding tragedy in that country.

HOWEVER, THE WORLD'S media have often been slow to report genocides. By the time the journalists and cameras arrive on the scene, hundreds of thousands of people may already be dead. This is mainly because the governments responsible for genocides take steps to keep their actions a secret, and journalists are often banned from the scene.

The latest edition of a Bosnian Serb newspaper, hot off the press. The media inside a country where a genocide takes place are often used as little more than mouthpieces for the dominant group, and can frequently inflame the situation.

When the world's media do get to report a genocide, its efforts to publicize the story, however well-intentioned, do not always have positive effects. Journalists don't always have an in-depth understanding of the background to a genocide, and this can lead to a distorted view of the situation. For example, early in the Bosnian conflict, most foreign journalists portrayed it as simply a flaring-up of age-old ethnic tensions. They did not mention Serbian aggression.

Many privately-owned, modern newspapers and TV stations look upon news stories partly as opportunities to increase their share of the audience or readership. Journalists are therefore encouraged to focus on the sensational aspects of a genocide – including images of starving or wounded victims – with less emphasis on informing people about the root causes.

This focus on the immediate crisis pressurizes governments and international agencies to respond with short-term solutions, such as helping victims with money, medical aid, and shelter. This aid is necessary and

A Western TV news crew film Hutu children in a refugee camp in Zaire in 1997. 'Human interest' stories tend to dominate media coverage of genocides. As a result, the viewer is often left feeling sympathetic but uninformed about the causes of the suffering.

helpful, but rebuilding a society following a genocide can take decades, and requires long-term solutions. Unfortunately, the media have a short attention span and, often within a few weeks, the world's cameras and microphones are pointing in a different direction, in another part of the world.

In some cases, it can be argued that the media can actually prepare a population for participation in a genocide. Newspapers in particular have been known to exploit the anxieties of certain sections of the public about the presence of a minority. In Britain, newspapers such as the *Daily Mail* and *Daily Express* have published negative reports about asylum seekers (people seeking refuge from persecution), claiming that many of them are illegal immigrants in search of a more comfortable life, and that they come here simply to claim benefits, to steal or to beg. These reports serve to reinforce a stereotype (a standard, oversimplified image) of asylum seekers in the public mind, and can be seen as the start of a process towards dehumanization.

Ignoring genocide

The American media have been criticized for not reporting on the genocide in Sudan in the 1980s and 90s: 'Americans know virtually nothing about Sudan. The American media ensure they know nothing... You are journalists. You know the code of journalism. Journalists cover events that are extraordinary... Events that set records. Sudan is full of records – awful, grisly records. Sudan is full of headlines – grim headlines. Yet American journalism largely ignores Sudan... Here is a headline: 2 million Sudanese people have died of war-related causes in the past 17 years... That's more war-related deaths than our own country has suffered during its entire history. That's not news?'

Source: Jeff Drumtra, US Committee for Refugees, 15 November 2000

How Does Genocide Affect People?

Genocides can affect individual victims as well as whole communities for years, even decades, after the killing has stopped. Survivors must cope with the loss of loved ones, and are often plagued by painful memories. They must try to rebuild their devastated lives, and deal with the practical issues of finding accommodation and food.

GENOCIDE SURVIVORS WHO lack the means to look after themselves or their families become refugees, dependent on the charitable activities of aid organizations. Some may be faced with injury or disfigurement as a result of wounds. The psychological scarring often never goes away, especially for child victims, and women who are raped during genocidal attacks.

Studies of Holocaust survivors have shown that virtually all suffered, to different degrees, from a condition known as 'survivor syndrome'. Symptoms included severe anxiety, losses of memory and understanding, depression and frequent illness. Most learned to live with their trauma, and managed to rebuild their lives, but others never recovered.

Tatars in traditional costume. The loss of their homeland through mass deportation meant the loss of institutions, such as schools, libraries, newspapers, museums and universities that were the storehouses of Tatar culture. This threatened the Tatars' very identity as a people.

Kurdish refugees fleeing from Iraqi troops in March 1991. Iraqi mass killings of Kurds – especially males – in the late 1980s and early 1990s, have left thousands of widows and orphans.

Many Cambodians remain, to this day, traumatized by the events of 1975–9. The stress caused by their memories of the genocide has sometimes led to physical illnesses, including blindness.

Genocides can also destroy whole communities. Following the genocide of the Hereros in 1904, the Germans took steps to ensure the tribe would never rise again. By making it illegal for them to own land or cattle, restricting their movements, and dispersing them across hundreds of different farms, the Hereros were given no opportunity to return to their traditional lifestyle or reorganize as a tribe. Most became labourers for German farmers, with no separate identity of their own.

The Armenians also lost their homeland, and very nearly their identity, as a result of the 1915 genocide. So many were killed that whole towns and villages disappeared from the map. For survivors, the forced removal from their homes meant the loss of everything they owned, leaving them penniless.

Hamid's story

Hamid, an Iraqi Kurd, was forced from his home in Kirkuk in 1997. He was visited by a government official who told him he had to go and live in a new modern village in a Kurdish area. No reason was given. His house, shop and farm were confiscated. The 'modern village' turned out to be a cramped, dusty settlement of grey cement houses and tents for 50 000 displaced Kurds. Hamid knew that the Iraqi government had moved him and the others because they were keen to take possession of oil-rich areas in and around Kirkuk. Arabs have now moved into Kirkuk, and taken over Hamid's property.

Source: BBC News, 3 November 2001

The effects of the Cambodian genocide are still felt today in the imbalance between the sexes. Because so many young men were killed, women – including many widows – make up 60 to 80 per cent of the adult population in many parts of Cambodia.

DEBATE - Does the mass deportation of a people from their homeland amount to a genocide?

- Yes. A people's identity is strongly bound up with where they live, and the loss of a homeland can mean the death of a culture.

- No. A people can survive the loss of a homeland. This cannot compare to the attempt to kill them.

The Armenians only survived as a people thanks to humanitarian aid from the USA. They were resettled in the Middle East, Russia and America, but the Armenians' historic bond with their homeland was lost forever.

The Ukrainian nation suffered in a similar way in 1932–3. Stalin ordered the seizure of all their farm produce because they had failed to meet food production targets. The famine that followed caused the deaths of between five and seven million people. The Ukrainian nation was crushed by this experience, their leadership was destroyed, and their language and culture clung on only in the countryside.

The Holocaust destroyed the once-thriving Jewish communities of eastern Europe. Hundreds of thousands of Jews, fearing anti-Semitism, decided not to return to their original homes after being liberated from the camps. Instead, many ended up going to Britain, America and Palestine.

Gypsies in Belzec extermination camp in Poland, 1942. Gypsies continued to face discrimination by German and Austrian police and welfare agencies after 1945. It was only in the 1980s that many gypsy survivors began to receive compensation for their sufferings.

Some victim communities can react to genocides by becoming more violent themselves, as happened to Bangladeshi society after the 1971 genocide. This peaceful community had traditionally resolved conflicts through negotiation and compromise. However, nine months of mass killing, rape and destruction had a brutalizing effect on the Bengali people. Students and young people became used to carrying arms and using violence to resolve disputes and settle scores. University campuses became the most dangerous places in the country.

A genocide inflicted by the Tutsis on the Hutus in Burundi in 1972, killing about 150 000 people, had a similar effect. The Hutus felt a violent anger towards the Tutsis, and a burning desire for revenge. This found its outlet in the 1994 genocide in Rwanda.

Genocide of the gypsies

As well as attempting to exterminate the European Jews, the Nazis also killed between a quarter and a half a million Roma and Sinti gypsies. Roma survivor Leopoldine Papai, interviewed in 1966, aged 36, gave this account:

'My parents were killed in Auschwitz, my father died of typhus... Shortly thereafter, my sister and I – together with many Jews – were sent to Ravensbruck. Many on this transport were shot, many died. After eight months, we were again deported ... to Bergen–Belsen. That was the worst. There was absolutely nothing to eat there and we slept on the bare ground. The British freed us in Bergen–Belsen. There are only two of us alive out of 36 family members; my sister and I... I have lung problems because of the camps and will probably never be completely healthy.'

Source: Century of Genocide: Eyewitness Accounts and Critical Views by Totten, Parsons and Charney (eds.)

Can Genocide Be Stopped?

The institutions set up to try to stop genocide – most notably the United Nations – have, so far, not succeeded in doing so. Many minorities around the world are still at risk of genocide. Effective methods of preventing genocides from happening in future need to be developed urgently.

MUCH RESEARCH HAS gone into the development of an effective genocide early warning system. The aim of such a system would be, firstly, to predict future genocides by looking out for the tell-tale signs, such as dehumanizing propaganda or the isolation of minorities. A network of organizations in a permanent state of readiness would be employed for this task.

Once a genocide has been predicted, the next task would be to investigate the allegations, probably by a UN office set up for this purpose. If the allegation

Sudanese refugees run to pick up food dropped by a United Nations plane. Through Operation Lifeline Sudan, the UN continues to give humanitarian aid to the suffering people of Sudan. However, the UN has been powerless to stop the continuing civil war in the country. In 2000, Sudanese government planes bombed a UN relief aircraft on the ground.

UN observers in Pakistan, where the Christian minority was facing increasing attacks by Islamic extremists in 2002. The UN needs to become better at anticipating genocides and preventing them from occurring.

The Dallaire fax

The need for a genocide early warning system was highlighted by the Rwandan genocide of 1994. In January 1994, the commander of the UN peacekeeping force in Rwanda, General Romeo Dallaire, sent a fax to UN headquarters, warning that genocide was being planned. The fax received a routine response, and no further action was taken. Other reports around this time, from diplomats and international organizations, also warned that ethnic tensions were rising. Despite this, the UN – and the world – were taken by surprise when, only months later, the massacres began.

proved difficult to establish. Firstly, genocides often take place during wars or revolutions, when the situation is chaotic and difficult for outsiders to observe or understand. Reports from refugees and eyewitnesses are not always reliable, and by the time objective international observers are in place, many thousands might already be dead. Sometimes, as in Indonesia in 1965, a genocide seems to start suddenly, with no clear warning. Therefore, one of the biggest challenges in trying to stop genocides is learning how to predict them.

How should we respond?

Once a genocide has been identified and the alert has been sounded, the next task is coaxing the international community to respond. Various levels of response are possible, usually beginning with an official protest to the guilty state. This is rarely effective, but at least serves warning that genocidal actions have been observed.

proves genuine, the media would be alerted to the developing crisis. Pressure would be applied on governments and international bodies to intervene and prevent the genocide from taking place.

Such a system sounds very good in theory, but for several reasons it has

UN peacekeeping troops in Bosnia. Ethnic tension between Serbs and Muslims continues, and international troops play an important role in preventing new conflicts emerging.

Victims or perpetrators?

Following the NATO campaign to end the Serb genocide against Albanian Muslims in Kosovo, reports began to surface of atrocities being carried out against Serbs by the Kosovo Liberation Army (KLA), an Albanian guerrilla group. This illustrates one of the risks of military intervention: action taken against perpetrators can encourage the victim group to retaliate with human rights violations of its own.

The next level of intervention is the use of sanctions (measures taken to place economic pressure on the government responsible), for example, by stopping trade with that country. Sanctions are usually slow to take effect, and can sometimes harden attitudes within the targeted government. They can also make life even harder for the threatened minority.

If sanctions fail to have an impact, a UN peacekeeping force may be sent in to try to stop massacres by separating the aggressors from their victims, establishing safety zones and protecting food supplies. Problems arise because peacekeeping forces are not authorized to fight, except in self-defence. They are, therefore, sometimes unable to prevent atrocities happening in front of them. This occurred, for example, in Srebrenica in Bosnia in 1995. Dutch peacekeeping troops surrendered 30 000 Muslim refugees to a Serbian force without resistance. A massacre of 7500 men and boys followed.

The most extreme form of intervention is military action. This is often the only effective way of bringing a halt to a genocide. However, the risks are great. There are likely to be deaths among the soldiers sent to intervene. Such operations are very expensive, and may lead to long-term involvement in the affected country. Establishing clear-cut military aims at the outset is therefore essential.

There is also the problem that in a conflict between ethnic groups, the issues are rarely black and white. In former Yugoslavia, for example, ethnic cleansing was carried out by the Croats as well as by the Serbs. So, before troops are committed, it is important to make clear where the guilt lies, who should be attacked, and who protected.

How is national interest a problem?

The main stumbling block that defeats most attempts at international action against genocide is national interest. Countries are often unwilling to take action in a situation where their national interest isn't directly at risk. Preventing a genocide in a distant region with which they have little commercial or strategic interest is often not high on their list of priorities.

DEBATE - Should foreign governments intervene militarily if they suspect a genocide is taking place within a certain country?

- Yes. The lives of innocent victims often depend on the prompt intervention of outside forces.
- No. We should not meddle in the internal affairs of other countries. How would you feel if foreign troops appeared on the streets of your country?

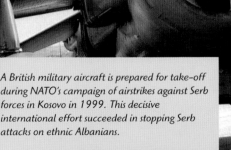

A British military aircraft is prepared for take-off during NATO's campaign of airstrikes against Serb forces in Kosovo in 1999. This decisive international effort succeeded in stopping Serb attacks on ethnic Albanians.

Rwandan women listen to the proceedings of a genocide trial in Kanombe district. A system of village courts has been set up in Rwanda, aimed at letting ordinary people judge those accused of killing their families and friends during the 1994 genocide.

Some countries actively oppose intervention when it is in their national interests to do so – if, for example, they have a strong trading relationship with the government carrying out the genocide. In 1975, Indonesia invaded East Timor and perpetrated a genocide that resulted in the deaths of around 350 000. Western nations did not respond, and the Western media did not wake up to the situation until around 1989. The genocide was ignored largely because Indonesia's oil reserves made it an important trading partner with the West.

What can the United Nations do?

The UN is the official forum where nations debate matters of international concern. Unfortunately, the UN is often unable to act effectively to counter genocide, mainly because member states cannot agree on what action should be taken. All UN intervention must first be approved by the five countries that make up the UN Security Council (China, France, Britain, Russia and the USA). Any of these countries has the power to veto (reject) the decisions of the others, effectively paralyzing the UN.

For example, in 1998, Serb forces were carrying out massacres, mass rapes and deportations in Kosovo. Russia, which has historic ties to Serbia, threatened to veto any UN military action. This forced NATO to intervene without UN Security Council approval, making its actions illegal under international law. Russia's attitude caused a delay and therefore further loss of life in Kosovo. This has led some to argue for an elimination of the veto, or a restriction of its use in genocidal situations.

Do trials work?

In 1945, Nazi perpetrators of the Holocaust were put on trial at Nuremberg. For the first time an international court was set up to prosecute individuals for crimes against humanity. Despite the UN's 1948 Genocide Convention making genocide illegal, no further international trials were held for almost 50 years. This was because the members of the UN were divided by the Cold War, and many governments refused to accept the legitimacy of an international court.

Then, in 1993, an International Criminal Tribunal (temporary court) was set up to try those responsible for the genocides in former Yugoslavia. A similar court was set up the following year to deal with the genocide in Rwanda. In July 2002, a permanent International Criminal Court (ICC) was created. Its purpose was to investigate and bring to justice individuals who commit genocide and other crimes against humanity.

East Timor

On occasion, UN intervention has been effective. After Indonesian troops went on the rampage in 1999, killing hundreds of East Timorese and causing more than 250 000 to flee into West Timor, the UN acted. An Australian-led force stabilized the country, and began preparing it for independence, which East Timor achieved in May 2002.

In East Timor, a UN investigator holds a cracked skull found in a mass grave. Approximately 60 bodies were unearthed, believed to have been killed by an armed militia supported by the Indonesian army in September 1999.

The progress of the tribunals has been slow and the trials have been costly. However, their establishment has sent out an important message. Any leaders contemplating genocide know that a system is now in place, and no one is immune from prosecution. This was made clear in 2001 when Slobodan Milosevic, the former president of Serbia, was brought to trial for his part in the genocide in Kosovo.

It is too early to say whether the trial process is effective, or whether it will act as a deterrent to future genocides. It is certainly important for genocide survivors to know that a system of justice exists. However, there is a danger that these trials may disrupt the natural healing processes of a community. Lengthy courtcases will keep the painful memories of the genocide fresh in the minds of those involved. This may fuel a desire for revenge, instead of allowing people to get on with rebuilding their lives.

Can we live together in peace?

What are the prospects of a world without genocide? The characteristics of hatred, fear and ruthlessness that drive people to commit this crime, show no signs of disappearing from human nature. So, prevention may be the only

Three Bosnian Serbs on trial for genocide sit behind their defence lawyers at the International Criminal Tribunal (ICT) in 1998. Being an international court with judges drawn from a range of different countries should mean that the ICC – the successor to the ICT – is less likely to be accused of bias.

cure. As well as introducing measures to stop current or impending (about to happen) genocides, as described in this chapter, governments and organizations must also look at ways of preventing genocides in the long term.

The key to this is education, especially in communities that have been damaged by genocide. Here young people are most at risk of getting sucked into a cycle of violence. They need to learn that all people, whatever their background, deserve respect. The common humanity and shared values of different cultures should be emphasized, by encouraging friendships between members of different communities, for example. It is also important to raise public awareness about past genocides.

Understanding the causes and effects of mass murder is one way of helping people to see its evil.

Some countries have managed to avoid potential genocide. In South Africa and Northern Ireland, for example, bitterly divided communities are learning to live in peace. It is not an easy path to follow when prejudices run so deep, but these examples at least offer hope that a future without genocide may be possible.

Dietrich Bonhoeffer, a Christian living in Nazi Germany, was an outspoken opponent of Nazi anti-Semitism. He was hanged by the Gestapo (Nazi secret police) in 1945 for trying to rescue Jews. Bonhoeffer remains an inspiring example of courage in the face of prejudice.

DEBATE - Should the people who carry out the killings be prosecuted for genocide, as well as the people who give the orders?

- Yes. It is no excuse for them to say that they were just carrying out orders. They are all equally guilty.
- No. Guilt lies with those who give the orders. If the executioners refuse, it is possible they may be killed themselves. Besides, others would certainly take their places.

REFERENCE

GENOCIDE IN THE TWENTIETH CENTURY

It has been estimated that nearly 170 million people were killed by governments in the twentieth century – roughly four times as many as were killed fighting in wars during the same period. Of these, approximately 83 million were killed in genocides, as defined by the United Nations (i.e. murdered because they belonged to a national, ethnic or religious group).

The states with the worst records of genocide and mass murder are as follows:

COUNTRY	YEARS	TOTAL (in 000s)
USSR	1917–87	61 911
People's Republic of China	1949–87	35 236
Germany	1933–45	20 946
China (Kuomintang)	1928–49	10 075
Japan	1936–45	5964
China (Mao Soviets)	1923–49	3468
Cambodia	1975–9	2035
Sudan	1956–2002	2000
Turkey	1909–18	1883
Vietnam	1945–87	1670
North Korea	1948–87	1663
Poland	1945–8	1585
Pakistan	1958–87	1503

Source: Power Kills, Rudolph Rummel, 1998

GENOCIDES SINCE 1945

The following table lists the major genocides and mass murders (involving the deaths of 50 000 or more) that have taken place since 1945.

Nation	Episodes	Estimated death toll/Victims	Main Perpetrators	Main Divisions
AFRICA				
Burundi	1959–62 1972 1988	200 000 Hutus 250 000 Hutus 50 000 Tutsis, 100 000 Hutus	Tutsi government and army	Ethnic and political
Congo	1994–2002	170 000 Hutus, Banyamulenge, Heme, Lendu	Ugandan, Rwandan, Congo armies	Racial, political, ethnic
Ethiopia	1945–74 1974–9	150 000 Oromo, Eritreans, Somalis 750 000 class enemies, Oromo	Selassie monarchy Dergue communists	National, religious Political, ethnic
Liberia	1990–2002	100 000 Krahn, Gio, Mano	Liberian government and army	Political, ethnic
Nigeria	1966–70	1 000 000 Ibos	Nigerian army	Political, ethnic, religious

Nation	Episodes	Estimated death toll/Victims	Main Perpetrators	Main Divisions
Rwanda	1994	800 000 Tutsi	Hutu government	Ethnic, political
Somalia	1988–2002	100 000 Somalis, Isaaq clan	Warlords, clan militias	Political, clan
Sudan	1956–2002	2 000 000 Nuer, Dinka, Christians Nuba, Southerners	Sudanese government	Political, religious, racial, ethnic
Uganda	1972–9	300 000 Acholi, Lango, Karamoja	Amin government and army	Political, ethnic, religious
	1980–6	250 000 Baganda, Banyarwanda	Obote government and army	

AMERICAS				
Brazil	1945–64	300 000 political enemies, Indians	Government, police, settler militias	Political, economic, ethnic
Guatemala	1950s–80s	200 000 Mayans	Government and army	Ethnic, political

ASIA				
Afghanistan	1996–2001	50 000+ Tajiks, Uzbeks, Hazara	Taliban	Political, religious, ethnic
Burma (Myanmar)	1962–78	100 000 Shan, Muslims, Karen, Christians	Burmese government	Ethnic, political, religious
Cambodia	1975–9	2 000 000 'class enemies', Cham Muslims, city people, Vietnamese, Eastern Zone	Khmer Rouge	Political, class, ethnic
China	1949–2002	35 000 000 'class enemies', religious minorities	Government, army, police	Political, ethnic, class, economic, national, religious
East Pakistan (Bangladesh)	1971	1 500 000 Bengalis, Hindus	Pakistani army	Political, national, ethnic, religious
East Timor	1975–2000	350 000 East Timorese	Indonesian army, militias	Political, ethnic, religious
Indonesia	1965	500 000 communists	Government	Political
North Korea	1949–2002	1 600 000 political enemies	Government, army,	Political, class
Tibet	1959–1990s	1 600 000 Tibetan Buddhists	Chinese government	National, political, religious
USSR	1945–91	15 000 000 'class enemies', nationalities, e.g. Karachai, Crimean Tatars, Balkar	Soviet government, army, secret police	Political, national, ethnic, religious
Vietnam	1954–75	1 670 000 class enemies, minorities	North Vietnamese government	Political, class, ethnic

Nation	Episodes	Estimated death toll/Victims	Main Perpetrators	Main Divisions
EUROPE				
Bosnia	1992–8	200 000 Muslims, Croats, Serbs	Bosnian Serbs, Croats	Ethnic, religious
Croatia	1991–5	50 000 Serbs, Bosnian Muslims	Croat army, militias	Ethnic, religious
Poland	1945–8	1 500 000 ethnic Germans	USSR government	Political

MIDDLE EAST				
Iran	1953–78 1978–92	260 000 government enemies 60 000 Kurds, monarchists, Bahai	Shah's secret police Iranian army	Religious, ethnic, political
Iraq	1961–2002	190 000 Kurds, Shiites, Kuwaitis	Iraqi government and army	Political, ethnic, national, religious
Lebanon	1974–91	55 000 Christians, Muslims, Druze	Religious militias	Religious, political

Source: Genocide Watch, Gregory Stanton, 2002

METHODS OF MASS MURDER

During the twentieth century, genocidal regimes used many different techniques for killing their citizens, including execution, forced labour and famine. The following table shows some different categories of genocide, and approximately how many people were killed in each category.

TYPE OF KILLING	NUMBERS KILLED
People murdered by their government	123 million
People murdered by a foreign government	39 million
People murdered in, or dying as a result of, incarceration in prisons or concentration camps	63 million
People murdered during, or dying as a result of, forced labour	58 million
Murder of specific individuals	34 million
Indiscriminate mass murder	23 million
Deaths as a result of famine inflicted by a regime	22 million
Deaths due to deportation or expulsion	8 million

Source: Power Kills, Rudolph Rummel, 1998

GENOCIDE WATCH

There are several international bodies dedicated to the work of monitoring potentially genocidal situations and human rights abuses. These include Amnesty International, International Alert, the Society for Threatened Peoples, the Genocide Prevention Center, the International Campaign to End Genocide, and the Genocide Research Center.

These organizations compile data by analysing reports from local media, governments, opposition groups and eyewitnesses, as well as using other surveillance techniques, in order to gain an accurate picture of the situation in areas where there are vulnerable minorities.

The following table lists countries where genocides were in progress or in danger of erupting in 2002.

Nation	Victims	Main Perpetrators	Main Divisions
AFRICA			
Burundi	Tutsi, Hutu	Tutsi government and army	Ethnic and political
Congo	Hutus, Banyamulenge, Heme, Lendu	Ugandan, Rwandan, Congo armies	Racial, political, ethnic
Liberia	Krahn, Gio, Mano	Liberian government and army	Political, ethnic
Nigeria	Tiv, Hausa, Yoruba, Ogoni, others	Nigerian army and police	Political, ethnic, religious
Somalia	Somalis, Isaaq clan	Warlords, clan militias	Political, clan
Sudan	Nuer, Dinka, Christians Nuba, Southerners	Sudanese government	Political, religious, racial, ethnic
Uganda	LRA enemies	Lord's Resistance Army	Political, ethnic, religious
Zimbabwe	White Europeans	Government, army, militias	Ethnic, political
AMERICAS			
Colombia	Political enemies	Marxists, right-wing death squads	Political
ASIA			
Afghanistan	Pashtun	Northern Alliance	Political, ethnic
Chechnya	Chechens	Russian army	National, ethnic, religious
China	'Class enemies', religious minorities	Government, army, police	Political, national, class, economic, ethnic, religious
India	Kashmiri Muslims	Hindu militias	National, religious, ethnic
Indonesia	Christians	Laskar Jihad	Ethnic, religious
North Korea	Political enemies	Government, army, police	Political, class
MIDDLE EAST			
Iraq	Kurds, Shiites	Iraqi government and army	Political, ethnic, national, religious

Source: Genocide Watch, Gregory Stanton, 2002

GLOSSARY

abduction Taking someone away by force.

anti-Semitism Prejudice against Jews.

atrocity A shockingly cruel act, usually involving violence.

classification The allocation of items (in this case people) to groups according to type.

Cold War The state of non-violent conflict between the Soviet Union and the United States and their respective allies between 1945 and 1990.

colony A country or region ruled by another country.

communism A system, or the belief in a system, in which capitalism is overthrown and control of wealth and property resides with the state.

concentration camp A prison camp used in war for the incarceration of political prisoners or civilians.

decapitate To cut off someone's head.

dehumanization The process of removing a person's or group's human qualities, in the eyes of others.

deportation The forcible removal of a person or people from a country.

economic depression A long period when trade is very slack, marked by high unemployment and poverty.

ghetto A run-down area of a city lived in by a minority group, especially a group experiencing discrimination.

guerrilla A member of an unofficial military force, usually with some political aim such as the overthrow of a government.

human rights The rights that are regarded by most societies as belonging to everyone, such as the rights to freedom, justice and equality.

humanitarian Committed to improving the lives of other people.

incarceration Imprisonment.

Islam The religion of Muslims, based on the teachings of the seventh-century prophet Muhammad.

Kuomintang The political party that ruled China from 1928 to 1947, until it was defeated by the Communists.

machete A large, heavy, broad-bladed knife used as a tool for cutting through vegetation, or as a weapon.

Mao Soviets Peasant councils created by Mao Zedong that controlled parts of rural China between 1923 and 1945.

Mesoamerica A region of Central America and southern North America that was occupied by several civilizations, especially the Maya and the Aztecs, before the arrival of the Europeans.

NATO The North Atlantic Treaty Organization, an international organization established in 1949 by the USA and Western Europe to promote international defence and collective security.

objective Free of any prejudice caused by personal feelings.

Ottoman Empire A Turkish empire established in the late thirteenth century in Asia Minor, eventually extending through the Middle East, which came to an end in 1922.

People's Republic of China The official name of communist China.

plantation A large estate or farm, especially in a hot country, where crops such as cotton, coffee, tea or rubber trees are grown.

polarization The process of exaggerating the differences between items (in this case people) so that those differences become ever more clear-cut and extreme.

propaganda Organized publicity, often by a government, to promote a particular view.

rape To force somebody to have sex.

refugee Someone who is seeking refuge, especially from war or persecution, by going to a foreign country.

repression The exertion of strict control over the freedom of others.

segregate To separate a person or group from the rest.

Soviet Union Also known as the USSR (Union of Soviet Socialist Republics), a country formed from the territories of the Russian Empire in 1917, which lasted until 1991.

symbolization The process of identifying a particular group with a symbol.

trauma An extremely distressing experience that can cause lasting psychological damage.

UN Security Council The permanent committee of the United Nations that oversees its peacekeeping operations around the world.

unsanitary Not clean.

World War I A war fought in Europe from 1914 to 1918, in which an alliance including Britain, France, Russia, Italy and the USA defeated the alliance of Germany, Austria-Hungary, Turkey and Bulgaria.

World War II A war fought in Europe, Africa and Asia from 1939 to 1945, in which an alliance including Britain, France, the Soviet Union and the USA defeated the alliance of Germany, Italy and Japan.

FURTHER INFORMATION

BIBLIOGRAPHY

Century of Genocide: Eyewitness Accounts and Critical Views
by Totten, Parsons and Charney (eds.)
(Garland Publishing, 1997)

Never Again: A History of the Holocaust
by Martin Gilbert
(Harper Collins, 2000)

A Witness to Genocide: The First Inside Account of the Horrors of Ethnic Cleansing in Bosnia
by Roy Gutman
(Element Books, 1993)

The Rape of Nanking: The Forgotten Holocaust of World War II
by Iris Chang
(Penguin Books, 1997)

Crimes Against Humanity: The Struggle for Global Justice
by Geoffrey Robertson
(Allen Lane, 1999)

ADDITIONAL SOURCES

Historical Atlas of the Twentieth Century
by Matthew White (2001)
[http://users.erols.com/mwhite28/warstat8.htm#Total]

Power Kills
by Rudolph Rummel (1998)
[http://www.hawaii.edu/powerkills/]

Genocide Watch, 2002
by Gregory Stanton
[http://www.genocidewatch.org/genocidetable.htm]

BOOKS

Judge For Yourself: Mao Zedong
by Christine Hatt
(Evans Books, 2002)

Survivors: A Story from Kosovo
by Stewart Ross
(Hodder Wayland, 2001)

Talking Points: Genocide
by R.G. Grant
(Hodder Wayland, 1998)

The Holocaust: Death Camps
by Pat Levy
(Hodder Wayland, 2000)

The Holocaust: Prelude to the Holocaust
by Jane Shuter
(Heinemann Library, 2002)

Troubled World: United Nations
by Ivan Minnis
(Heinemann Library, 2001)

Troubled World: Wars of Former Yugoslavia
by Ivan Minnis
(Heinemann Library, 2001)

Twentieth Century Leaders: Stalin
by Peter Chrisp
(Hodder Wayland, 2002)

WEBSITES

**www.historyplace.com/worldhistory/
genocide**
Accounts of some of the major
genocides of the twentieth century.

www.amnesty.org
The website of Amnesty International,
a pressure group working to protect
human rights worldwide.

www.endgenocide.org
The website of the Campaign to End
Genocide.

www.genocide.be
The website of the Genocide Research
Center.

www.preventgenocide.org
The website of Prevent Genocide
International.

www.genocideprevention.org
The website of the Center for the
Prevention of Genocide.

www.genocidewatch.org
The website of Genocide Watch.

www.aegistrust.org
The website of the Aegis Trust, a
genocide prevention initiative.

INDEX